This book belongs to

Norman Rockwell's
American Memories

MJF BOOKS

NEW YORK

Frontispiece: AT THE SODA FOUNTAIN
Saturday Evening Post cover, August 22, 1953

Published by MJF Books
Fine Communications
Two Lincoln Square
60 West 66th Street
New York, NY 10023

Norman Rockwell's American Memories
Library of Congress Catalog Card Number 99-74468
ISBN 1-56731-352-3

This volume includes three books formerly published as *American Memories-Norman Rockwell, Wit and Humor of Norman Rockwell,* and *An American Family Album-Norman Rockwell,* all copyright © 1993 by Armand Eisen.

Printed in Singapore on acid-free paper

MJF Books and the MJF colophon are trademarks of Fine Creative Media, Inc.

10 9 8 7 6 5 4 3 2 1

MENDING THE FLAG

Literary Digest cover
May 27, 1922

THE OPEN ROAD

Saturday Evening Post cover
July 31, 1920

THE DEBATE

Saturday Evening Post cover
October 9, 1920

HALLOWEEN

Saturday Evening Post cover
October 23, 1920

POSTCARD

———

Saturday Evening Post cover
February 18, 1922

SPEED

Saturday Evening Post cover
July 19, 1924

THE TACKLE

Saturday Evening Post cover
November 21, 1925

UNCLE SAM TAKES WING

———

Saturday Evening Post cover
January 21, 1928

FISHING

Saturday Evening Post cover
August 3, 1929

STOCK EXCHANGE QUOTATIONS

Saturday Evening Post cover
January 18, 1930

FIRE!

Saturday Evening Post cover
March 28, 1931

CRAMMING

Saturday Evening Post cover
June 13, 1931

THE SPIRIT OF EDUCATION

Saturday Evening Post cover
April 21, 1934

STRIKING A BARGAIN

Saturday Evening Post cover
May 19, 1934

VACATION

Saturday Evening Post cover
June 30, 1934

SCHOOL DAYS

Saturday Evening Post cover
September 14, 1935

BARBERSHOP QUARTET

Saturday Evening Post cover
September 26, 1936

FIRST FLIGHT

—

Saturday Evening Post cover
June 4, 1938

THE DRUGGIST

Saturday Evening Post cover
March 18, 1939

100 YEARS OF BASEBALL

—

Saturday Evening Post cover
July 8, 1939

CENSUS TAKER

Saturday Evening Post cover
April 27, 1940

USO VOLUNTEERS

Saturday Evening Post cover
February 7, 1942

ROSIE THE RIVETER

Saturday Evening Post cover
May 29, 1943

WHICH ONE?

———

Saturday Evening Post cover
November 4, 1944

TAXES

Saturday Evening Post cover
March 17, 1945

HAPPY HOMECOMING

Saturday Evening Post cover
May 26, 1945

THANKSGIVING

Saturday Evening Post cover
November 24, 1945

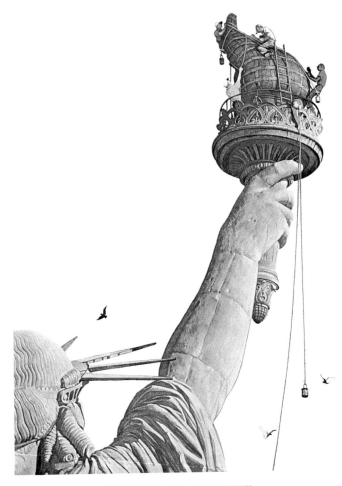

STATUE OF LIBERTY

Saturday Evening Post cover
July 6, 1946

ELECTION DAY

—

Saturday Evening Post cover
October 30, 1948

BOTTOM OF THE SIXTH

Saturday Evening Post cover
April 23, 1949

EXPENSES

Saturday Evening Post cover
November 30, 1957

THE RUNAWAY

Saturday Evening Post cover
September 20, 1958

SAYING GRACE

———

Saturday Evening Post cover
November 24, 1951

FRAMED

Saturday Evening Post cover
March 2, 1946

THE BODY BUILDER

Saturday Evening Post cover
April 29, 1922

BEDSIDE MANNER

—

Saturday Evening Post cover
March 10, 1923

THE CRITIC

———

Saturday Evening Post cover
July 21, 1928

THE PIE THIEF

Saturday Evening Post cover
August 18, 1928

SERENADE

Saturday Evening Post cover
September 22, 1928

THE GOSSIPS

—

Saturday Evening Post cover
January 12, 1929

TRAVELER

Saturday Evening Post cover
July 13, 1929

NO SWIMMING

Saturday Evening Post cover
June 15, 1929

JAZZ IT UP

Saturday Evening Post cover
November 2, 1929

PRACTICING

Saturday Evening Post cover
November 7, 1931

CHILD PSYCHOLOGY
—

Saturday Evening Post cover
November 25, 1933

HANG ON!

———

Saturday Evening Post cover
July 13, 1935

THE NANNY

Saturday Evening Post cover
October 24, 1936

SEE THE WORLD

Saturday Evening Post cover
April 24, 1937

DOLORES AND EDDIE

Saturday Evening Post cover
June 12, 1937

THE ANTIQUE HUNTER

Saturday Evening Post cover
July 31, 1937

WET PAINT!

———

Saturday Evening Post cover
October 2, 1937

FIRE!

Saturday Evening Post cover
May 27, 1944

THE JESTERS

Saturday Evening Post cover
February 11, 1939

THE SPORTING LIFE

Saturday Evening Post cover
April 29, 1939

SHERIFF AND PRISONER

Saturday Evening Post cover
November 4, 1939

THE WORKS!

Saturday Evening Post cover
May 18, 1940

SCHOOLGIRL

—

Saturday Evening Post cover
March 1, 1941

THANKSGIVING DAY

Saturday Evening Post cover
November 28, 1942

PLAYING CHECKERS

Saturday Evening Post cover
April 3, 1943

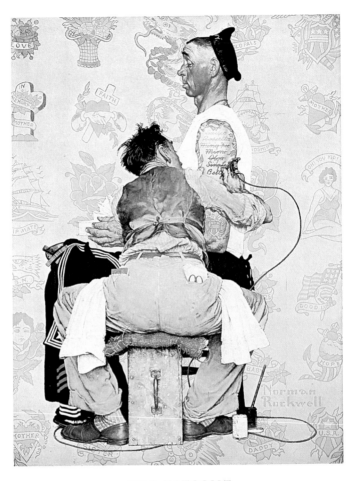

THE TATOOIST

Saturday Evening Post cover
March 4, 1944

APRIL FOOL'S

—

Saturday Evening Post cover
March 31, 1945

THE HAPPY GARDENER

Saturday Evening Post cover
March 22, 1947

BABYSITTING

Saturday Evening Post cover
November 8, 1947

THE DIETER

—

Saturday Evening Post cover
January 3, 1953

FEEDING TIME

Saturday Evening Post cover
January 9, 1954

A FAIR CATCH

Saturday Evening Post cover
August 20, 1955

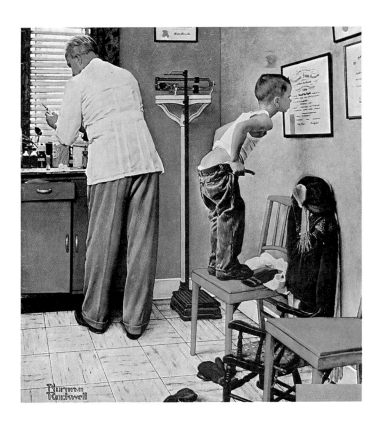

AT THE DOCTOR'S

Saturday Evening Post cover
March 15, 1958

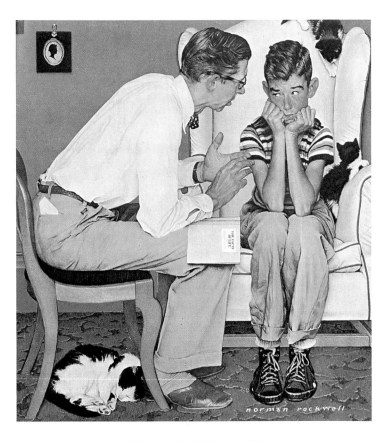

THE FACTS OF LIFE

—

Saturday Evening Post cover
July 14, 1951

GRANDPA AT BAT

—

Saturday Evening Post cover
August 5, 1916

NO SWIMMING

—

Saturday Evening Post cover
June 4, 1921

GRANDPA AND CHILDREN

Literary Digest cover
December 24, 1921

THE ACCOMPANIST

Saturday Evening Post cover
February 3, 1923

DOCTOR AND DOLL

———

Saturday Evening Post cover
March 9, 1929

HOME FROM VACATION

Saturday Evening Post cover
September 13, 1930

CRAMMING

———

Saturday Evening Post cover
June 13, 1931

GOING OUT

Saturday Evening Post cover
October 21, 1933

CHILD PSYCHOLOGY

Saturday Evening Post cover
November 25, 1933

VACATION

Saturday Evening Post cover
June 30, 1934

THE GIFT

Saturday Evening Post cover
January 25, 1936

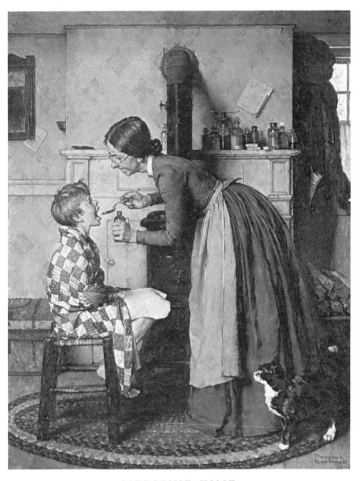

MEDICINE TIME

Saturday Evening Post cover
May 30, 1936

THE NANNY

Saturday Evening Post cover
October 24, 1936

THE COLD

Saturday Evening Post cover
January 23, 1937

DREAMBOATS

Saturday Evening Post cover
February 19, 1938

FIRST FLIGHT

Saturday Evening Post cover
June 4, 1938

AT THE BEACH

Saturday Evening Post cover
July 13, 1940

A SCOUT IS HELPFUL

Boy's Life cover
February, 1942

BACK FROM CAMP

—

Saturday Evening Post cover
August 24, 1940

FAMILY OUTING

Saturday Evening Post cover
August 30, 1947

IT'S GOOD TO BE HOME!

———

Saturday Evening Post cover
December 25, 1948

PROM DRESS

Saturday Evening Post cover
March 19, 1949

PRACTICE

Saturday Evening Post cover
November 18, 1950

FOUR SPORTING BOYS: BASEBALL

Brown & Bigelow
1951 Four Seasons Calendar, Spring

AT THE VET'S

Saturday Evening Post cover
March 29, 1952

WALKING TO CHURCH

Saturday Evening Post cover
April 4, 1953

GIRL IN THE MIRROR

Saturday Evening Post cover
March 6, 1954

LEAVING HOME

Saturday Evening Post cover
September 25, 1954

THE LOST TOOTH

Saturday Evening Post cover
September 7, 1957

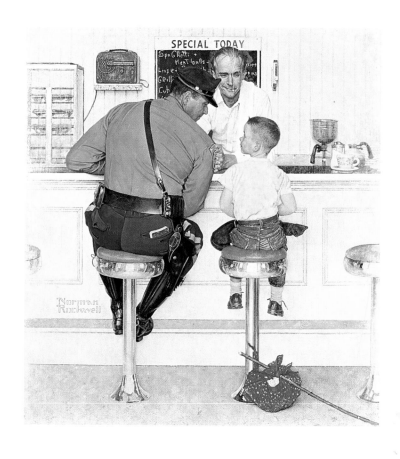

THE RUNAWAY

Saturday Evening Post cover
September 20, 1958

THE GRADUATE

Saturday Evening Post cover
June 6, 1959

GUESTS ARRIVING AT A PARTY

Saturday Evening Post cover
August 7, 1920

FAMILY GRACE

———

Ladies' Home Journal
August, 1938